ROAMING CHARGES

ROAMING CHARGES
Antony Di Nardo

Brick Books

Library and Archives Canada Cataloguing in Publication

Di Nardo, Antony, 1949–, author
    Roaming charges / Antony Di Nardo.

Poems.
Issued in print and electronic formats.
ISBN 978-1-77131-348-3 (pbk.).—ISBN 978-1-77131-350-6 (pdf).—ISBN 978-1-77131-349-0 (epub)

    I. Title.

PS8607.I535R63 2015   C811'.6   C2014-907843-9
                                           C2014-907844-7

We acknowledge the Canada Council for the Arts, the Government of Canada through the Canada Book Fund, and the Ontario Arts Council for their support of our publishing program.

The author photo was taken by Ann Nadin.
The book is set in Sabon.
Cover image by René Mansi.
Design and layout by Marijke Friesen.

Printed and bound by Sunville Printco Inc.

Brick Books
431 Boler Road, Box 20081
London, Ontario N6K 4G6

www.brickbooks.ca

for

Callie, Isaac, and Lucas

CONTENTS

Auto-Bouquet /3

I
Roaming Charges—Big Deal, Beirut /7
The Lilies of an Arab Spring /8
Hamra /9
Let Heaven and Nature Sing /10
Sunday in a Square in Aleppo /11
Satisfaction /13
The Terrible Fires of Retribution Burned and Burned,
 but Beirut Held Up /14
Like No Other Place /15
Ignite /16
The Next Big War /18
Ballad from the Back of the Bus /19
No Reason /20
Gunflowers /21
Card Sharps /22
Naval Patrol /23
Dead Pigeon Poem /25
Etherized /26
I Can't Live Here /27
Probe /29
The Good Song /30

II
Roaming Charges—Digs /33
Don't Look Back /34
The Hat /35
Twitterpated /37
Museum Pieces: Galleria Borghese /38
Desktop /40
The Writing Life /41
Manhattan Flattened: After the Sack of Rome /42

A Look Inside Cy Twombly's *Second Voyage to Italy* /43
Woman Declining Stairs (Suicide Bomber #2) /44
Daphne and Apollo: A Study Typed in Sentences /46
PAINTER, Painter /47
Rosa Rosa Vagabonda /48
Remus, the Forgotten One /49
(Witness) /50
The Disquieting Muses /51
Byron's Missing Fingers: Lessons from the Imagists /52

III
Roaming Charges—"Land Over Landings" /57
Echo Lake /58
Can't Complain (Just Look at Detroit) /59
Coming in Friday to Windsor on Wednesday /60
Envoy /61
The Tower /62
Toying with the Above /63
In and Out of Chatham /64
The Air in the Bus /65
London 2012 /66
Pax Canadensis /67
The National Pantry /68
Three Balconies /69
Poets on a Plane /71
   August Kleinzahler /71
   Michael Ondaatje /72
   Mary Oliver /73
   Erin Mouré /74
   Carmine Starnino /75
   Ken Babstock /76
   James Tate /77
North of Cochin /78

Notes and Acknowledgments /81
Biographical Note /85

But people change, they grow up, they fly around.

—*James Tate*

Auto-Bouquet

I was never born in Italy. Not even once.

Where I landed, sidewalks bore my name stamped in concrete taken from the borders between heaven and earth. I made light of hell, bent brooms for the blind to sweep away the dark. Like my father and his father before him.

I collected blood samples for the church divinity. The bread we broke was not our bread, touched by the hands of butchers and train engineers.

We lived for the altered states of the only begotten son on a street named Dante.

A cross, across from Our Lady of the Minister of Defense, matched the cruciform shadows of flights overhead.

I listened to grandfather's clarinet on the feast day of Francis, the saint who sang for the birds at the helm of the crowds.

I remember the wars that never came. Only the ghosts of war. The unidentified contrails. And the Sunday drill to the fallout shelters.

I loved ice cream as a child but I couldn't understand it.

It wouldn't stay.

I grew, like most men my age, out of a flowerpot.

I

Roaming Charges—Big Deal, Beirut

And the beast breaks its back on a Benjamin. No change expected.

Erstwhile, a single-shot salute. Pigeons, barely born, walk to work on a ledge. Things get moving. Iterate. And the beautiful silk of the day goes unnoticed, while bells and minarets ring another audio rooftop formula. The Corniche, for all to see, is wash-and-wear. And the men you hate to hate are never there, busy behind downtown doors.

They talk of borders, the world beyond, memory as the long and short of it. They talk in circles, city squares, then vaporize. It's the climate that keeps them here.

Bursts of bougainvillea, explosive RPGs. Like any big bang, the results are gone in a matter of days. Or last a lifetime on a couch. Missing fingers, legs lost at the breach, that's normal. What you don't see coming can't hurt you is what they say.

Well, not quite—the back of a bullet-t-t-t-t just now jammed on the tip of my tongue.

The Lilies of an Arab Spring

All hail the prescient light of the sun
overwhelming the daze of burgeoning
canna lilies on our back balconies,
spears of outward show to mask
the purple bud within. Such days
belong to the uptick of freedoms,
a brace of petals up in arms,
a time to state a people's argument,
integument of stalk and stem burst forth
on china set for millions at the table.
The multitudes and married look-alikes,
the alabaster homing pigeons honed
to make it back every time they leave,
these too are on their mark and set to go.

Hamra

can't wait to have us back. The cafés aren't much but simple to sit at. Think of yourself in a robe. Money never goes hungry here. The billboards beg. Service taxis sweat doing double time to a Mideast *dabke* version of "La Mer." The best of Beirut going seaside where nothing can escape any further from the cut-out chatter of one-legged traffic.

We're deep in the heart of a demilitarized zone. "Fa-la-la!" we sing and pull down the screen (ready-made words read in loops from right to left), and the sky we see is shocked to be the way it's always been. Oh, how we walked and strutted—roamed the streets of stairways going up, your fearsome fowl-step to cover ground.

Now at the Duke of Wellie we stand time on its head, happy hour leaking down our throats, the city pearled and peopled.

I hear they're tunnelling underneath this part of the world again and they've put another face on a stamp. Moles, miles beneath our feet, dig deep, and the city swells just outside the tents in a high-rise, heads above the minarets, where ignorant armies clash by night.

Let Heaven and Nature Sing
   —after Naharnet's Live News website (Beirut, December 9, 2012)

Two soldiers and two civilians were wounded in a mortar shell attack on an army position in the Talaat al-Omari area in Tripoli.

The army dismantled an explosive in the Tall area in Tripoli.

Explosions caused by rocket fire were heard in Tripoli.

Fierce clashes renewed amid reports of two deaths in Tripoli.

Gunfire exchange resumed in the areas of Al-Qamh market, Al-Hara, Al-Barraniyeh, Al-Sayyida, Starco, and Jabal Mohsen in Tripoli.

The bodies of the men killed in Tall Kalakh will be returned in several batches to Tripoli.

An Energa-type grenade fell on Syria Street and the army is responding to gunfire sources in Tripoli.

Sniper gunfire wounded Mohammed al-Hamouyi from the Bab al-Tabbaneh neighbourhood and Ghanem Hasan from the Jabal Mohsen neighbourhood in the northern city of Tripoli.

Those who lose, he said, are blasphemous and take Allah's name to Tripoli.

Sunday in a Square in Aleppo

Satellite dishes on other people's rooftops convey the daily stars that turn and speak to me and the mosque master's voice also speaks to me bypassing Allah and the good intentions that I must face

and in the square, the only square in Aleppo where the sun can beat unhampered, where pepper trees can breathe and the palm trees belong, I sit and watch two boys throw dice into a gaming box and they surround the click of dice with a little conversation

and I'm stunned by the rapid rhythms of their hands, their calculations, while behind them the pigeons swoop across the paving stones and come up empty

and the shoe-shine boy with the imperial head is impervious to my refusals and today is Sunday and it's December and the air has warmed itself to this

and a man who walks around the square stops to let the locals kiss him on both cheeks and he has Down's syndrome and the boys interrupt their game to kiss him too

and another man is barking leather coats for sale and someone else is looking for another pair of shoes to shine and this day in December sets its own tableau

of people's faces, people's voices muted by a winter light upon the lightness of the paving stones, as silver and slow as any city ever gets without the crushing blows it takes outside this square

with the street lamps leaning and the palms and pepper trees and silver shops and cafés and the foreign voices that are mostly men in their Sunday best of coloured scarves sitting on the benches in this square in Aleppo that is not Carré Saint-Louis or Place des Vosges or Washington Square, but Saahat al-Hattab

and that means Yaqoub, the silversmith, is lost in his shop and that's the bakery that was opened yesterday but closed today and the men who crowded at its ancient worn-out windows are gone

and little remains of the whitewashed trunk of the plane tree that occupies the centre of the square, its crown cut down, its limbs removed, stumps where once its leafy mane topped the square and shaded those who sat around its summer skirt, listening as I do now

to the click of dice and the sounds of men and their footsteps across the paving stones fading into a simple geometric quietude of birds and winter light and all of this accumulation of the world in a city on a Sunday silvered in Aleppo.

Satisfaction

It's 4:00 or 5:00 PM in the Middle East and if the sky was a giant blackboard we'd all be up on rooftops blurring out the mess of winter clouds we made today, the sunset scribbled in as an afterthought.

Instead I'm caught between Mick Jagger's "Satisfaction" plugged into my ears and the speakers of the evening muezzin perched like doves in his minaret

coo-coo-cooing the many names of Allah—one voice feeding on the other until both sound so much alike I sing along.

The Terrible Fires of Retribution Burned and Burned, but Beirut Held Up

Summer was loud but loved.

Thunderclaps way above decibel breaking glass beneath the rooftops.

We had a time of it, lots on our minds, attitudes to burn, that summer of one explosion after another.

The beaches suffered wide wide gashes and were left abandoned.

Towns and towers collapsing right on target, you could see it coming, but what could one do other than wait for it to blow over?

The sea still swayed like hips on the once-young women of Hamra, lovely angels all the same, well before Allah came for them, wrapped each in swaddling clothes, and dropped them in a deep deep hole.

We called him Allan, the man up there, for the fun of it, but there was nothing funny about him when he got down to work.

Like No Other Place

The sweat of some men. Of bar stools and camels busy on the beach. Of happiness on Bliss Street.

There's such a disproportionate call for acquittals, for silence, for the ancient walls to be dismantled, I can't make up my mind where to look.

Women dressed in shrouds of armour nakedly in black appear.

How bicycles don't appear.

In lieu of peace, chipped coffee cups and café gods, hints of immortality in every demitasse consumed.

In lieu of praise, the high holy days.

How the final hour gets fixed in time is a mystery, as it is in heaven.

How the swing of the pen brings the minaret along with the men who man it.

Then one day—was it the window dressing? was it the pearl in the wink of a moon?—I held your hand as we faced the sea and felt the supreme longing of a warm summer's eve.

Ignite

The sky's so wasted, dark and blue, indigo and glow, there's nothing else to see.

The dinner plates rattling well past seven could be breakfast's last turn at the sink.

Sticks, stones, breaking bones, the snapping sounds of all utilitarian needs.

Tires' indiscriminate screech and squeal. The world is round.

Doors slam, reiterate. Something somewhere happens here.

Voices like a paper bag wrestle with a wayward wind.

Cars in compromising contradictions take turns rolling in reverse.

Motors. Heat. Rooftop drums, generators beating out the heat.

A cough as thick as men outside these walls.

The reach and muscle of those on foot.

Of troubled waters.

The reach of keys.

The breach of smoke and cigarettes.

A gun salutes the not-too-distant past.

The truth of being on the roof.

The day ends here.

Two streets over, *centre ville*.

Downtown, the sea in flames.

The Next Big War

You find among the meagre helpings that wash up on
the national shores: baby bottles, plastic bottles, and other
people's empty buckets (their lists only partially ticked off,
never having made it to the other coast or stepped
in traffic with the right amount of horsepower).

In the papers, news reports, mediated broadcasts,
Mary is still the virgin of record.
Elvis bears a grudge.
The world is a big and beautifully dismayed blue pearl.

You hear the next big war is just around the corner:
sighs and tripods, bodies made of Kevlar,
the global hit parade gleaming on a stack of foreheads.

Briefly on the cable channels a different planet comes into view,
pitted with bubbles and tender quips, a home without
doors or similar household inventions tagged
with life-supporting Third-World flags.
A place of palaces without the guardrails for the masses.

A city we know too well comes out to play
a game of shock and awe, accolades for the camouflage.
Another city dreams itself a shoreline with a boat for two,
a carousel on weekends, the wild discovery that it's
always been self-contained, immured, and fortified.

Again today, the genius of mortality nails to a blank
and empty wall these words—
Before, this too was just a wall—fitted to a certainty
of knowing who's got the better brain. A crane swings full circle.
The square empties out.
Those who wait for war have been duly disenchanted.
The others park their cars.

Ballad from the Back of the Bus

Christ you know it ain't easy,
sang the boy in the band,
there are gunmen on every corner.

A child goes out to play, comes back
gun-mad, god-crazed,
simple-minded.

If you don't like what you see, you
stay away. Find a cause. Go pack an RPG.
So say the laws of man-made laws.

You start out seminal, then you're on your own,
at risk, like any other who's on the brink.
Dirt cheap. Nothing stays for very long.

But a father on a bus with his three children
who points out the horror of a roadside tank,
armed and manned,

awful breach
of love and peace, now there's someone
who'd take a bullet for you.

No Reason

The muezzin who sings at the top of his lungs, sings and penetrates the clouds beneath a vanishing sky.

His voice reaches all that's meant to be, a miracle of ubiquity, and the minarets are just about everywhere too.

One voice, for sure, so high and mighty.

Then the bats come out, swinging, and swallowing every word they hear. Every word that hangs in the lofty air is theirs to keep.

And I hear the sounds of Manhattan beneath the sky. And those of Montreal's are beneath the ground. And those that ring on the platforms of Paris are quickly gone, as are those at the feet of New Delhi and the words on the beaches of Puntarenas that all come together in the reach of the one minaret and the steeple bells too and the dusk and the wings and the night above all.

Gunflowers

In like-minded valleys the world over,
Okanagan abundance, storehouse of vitamins A,
B, and C, the daily study of the sun that shoots its rays
in multiples of goodness, happiness,

all under one roof and, oh, its ever-giving GDP,
so unlike the kindness of the Mideast sky that shifts
its gaze over to one side of the Med and sees deflected
the bright intentions of country life, the rockets'

red glare redirected as inexplicable bombs let go.
And in the arc from East to West, the Bekaa Valley
carves a curse, the sun keeps on its
steady course, war drums beating down the crops,

the bodies of instant warriors pulverized
to nitrogen and nutrients, all the letters of their names
rearranged so you can't make sense of who they were
or ever get to know what the sun has been up to.

Card Sharps

Big rocks portend bigger rocks. Cockfights settle the biggest dick.

Shudder the humanity, but now and forever on the freeway to the Dead Cities, Syria on the verge of dying deserts, men with guns exposed, appalled that other men should go without them.

The clans wake up to cross-and-crescent battles, dialectics, sordid Bradley tanks that roller-coaster craters into every city street.

Big can break a world in two real quick, take apart a wall someone carried on his back for years, the road into his pockets empty.

Tough shit. The Bristol board placards block the gates. It's always been the reign of *Rex* and rules, card sharps ever since—clubs and spades, hearts and diamonds, the four pillars of all big dreams, all big dreams that dare.

Naval Patrol

Some star flickered lightbulb-like and then went out without a word.

A match was a striking resemblance and served as plain as day.

Cargo-shipping lanes wet with goods went by.

Lips lost at shore became the call of the Corniche escaping.

It's a lie, it's alive, frothing from the sea.

There's little doubt some men downtown are big in debt.

An heirloom halo for the stars at night, right where we had left it.

Billboards aging, sagging chins.

Mid-year crisis. The world looks back and sees it's always been the same.

Tuna on toast, a photogenic whale gone missing.

And, oh, the canaries of Times Square lingering by the banks of empty bookshelves.

Please come by the bar, the greengrocer's hat and his dandelion salad are still there.

Next to the necktie the growl of a man in matching lapels.

Chico's DVD Emporium scarred and yellowed by satellites and instant downloads.

Gun smoke, pot smoke stuck in the lungs of the city.

What bouquet of trees can surpass this crowd of jacaranda, fig, and pomegranate all at once?

Nobody knew the mentally fit were for the good of the realm as well.

Like an argument dissolves on the tip of the tongue. Hard candy.

Our eyes, I've noticed, are terribly fond of each other.

Dead Pigeon Poem

Poor thing, popped on flat-top roof, pigeon's-eye view of the mourning sky, middle of a Mideast state and how did I ever get here.

A window writes itself into the view with a sudden burst of light.

Heavenly, October by the Med, when one sky fits all.

A fit of passion with a pen? You bet!

I'll take that any day over whatever's burning in a gunman's head. The bullet packed, the barrel aimed, all god's children simulating pigeons popped-up-in-a-row, life both deep and cheap.

And right over there, right there, that man sitting at the window just cocked his gun and picked my brain.

Etherized

You might spark a revolution,
read a book,
sit down for takeout turkey dinner on your own,
the Arab Spring your favorite episode of the year,
the channel changer firmly in your grip—
a way of keeping up
to days' demands, etherized
the moment you get things done.

One might wish a falling star,
pray for rain,
hope against all hope,
but for all we know nothing
will curtail or alteration bring
tomorrow's gift of daylight, nighttime's respite,
or pen-and-paper platitudes
that report the Sunday news for years to come.
Que será, será in deed and thought,
the future's not ours to see,
so cut yourself some slack
and put your mind at ease, Time's the patient
on the table. Call me back next week.

I Can't Live Here

To stay frightens me as much as leaving does.

By the time I found out the evening and morning stars were just about the same, Venus was already a planet.

You live, you die, you bake an apple pie.

You love the symphony for its jazz.

Dogs are frightful beasts. Like dragons, they lunge and catch your breath. Mudgett Road is peppered with them.

At Maria's gate the linden trees made lemonade for the sun.

The little Frost that I remember, woodpiles, moon pies, tell a story I knew as a child, stacks of small perfections. Rearrangements. Putting together a cv.

The house, to flex a muscle, puts all birds on a budget. The mourning dove as raptor.

Segolène is a French woman's name. *Érablière* is an arrow off the sign. *Ashrafiyeh* is the little mountain where someone lives.

The three principles of rock paper scissors, all you need to win or lose.

And it's a spin of limbs, that boy chasing a ball across the road.

As great and green a meadow, God's great green handkerchief, was said of Central Park.

I see best when I look over mountaintops.

Silos for the farmer's tillage, black-and-white meadow cows. I'm almost there.

I gather feathers. I move on. I gather more.

A single sock represents another life on earth.

A few more steps.

The road begins to climb.

Probe

Pigeon No. 2 basking in a column of diminishing light. I'm thinking opposites of rain, the sharpened blade that disappears a little with every sharpening that it takes. Brick of moon, veined or veiled, it's all the same to me. Blood feuds at closing time. One-way streets, lichened green and grey, one-way rivers floating to a stolen sea. Down the drain. Satellite prompts and digital cons. Cable visionaries. Co-cohesion. Renaissance of the rooftop garden thatched in bloom. Publican springs. Outweighed opinions way way out and out o' the way. October by the Med. Bullet shells swept from out of sight. Outta sight. Out of recon. Plush brain pellets. Cellular thoughts. Rehab of the upholstered mind. Gun belts. Bible belts. Koranic pelts and feathers for the heist of the sacrifice. Bird on the wing? Where else? The sky a constant goofy goodbye.

The Good Song

It's *tempus fuckit* at Café Younes,
west of Babylon and east of yesterday,
where I hang a left at the Commodore Hotel
and succumb to the common nonsense.

A mile away they're up to something quite unthinkable.
War shoves a finger in your eye
while you read about it
and never goes away.

But the city's still intact
with its summer spread of salt-and-pepper look-alikes at the tables.
You see, it was the bombing that survived and, despite the roadworks,
the radar of sudden departures,

there was still some hope we'd all be hale and wholesome,
hanging on the bright side, happy at the end of our tether.

II

Roaming Charges—Digs

T ex t f r om a   p   age in a ro om   by D on De L illo—

Every so often I'd stop and look up and see a sky that seemed confined, compressed.

That seemed confused.

Now read it back to me.

The sky stretched taut between two places I had been.

At the height of where I am.

On the brink of where I was.

Don't Look Back

We had a moment or two
at a picnic, her tresses tangled
with mine, and only last night
the fever of a moon directing traffic
through both our eyes. Coincidence?
Perhaps, but we'd been looking
in the same direction for such
a long time a painter of the nineteenth
century was bound to know
where we were. And when
we stepped out into the dimming
light of the public gardens,
plane trees, chestnuts, and oaks
at the gates, Orpheus glued
to his lute, a perimeter of pansies
in meaningful thoughts, she left
for the coast in a cab and I leaned
on the rail of a bridge in a work
by the very same artist.

The Hat

To tear a denim sky in two and reach for a beer.
To hang on a common thread. The city grins,
a face at my window falling just like Galileo

predicted. Audubon too predicted birds flying blindly
into each other. I keep gathering feathers
on the edge of a realm where she passed by.

Curfews on the midnight hustle. Curses on the destitute
of tongue. Of countryside. They stood me years ago
in a corner of a cereal box without her anywhere

in sight. It was at the time of the big bleak and the nuns.
They fed us milk through straws. One opened
desks like clams and fed them hooks and capers,

college scores and sardine tins. Prehensile once, as in I touched
her heart and there it all began. On the last day, a jubilee
of fireflies danced until midnight before they left for good.

I touched her bank account, her hair, the apples rotting
underneath the sink. I touched the timpani she played.
Bluebirds caged, gods unleashed, canaries, all

made a slight impression. We've split, but hell, we don't have
to bend like that ever again. Yes, there once was a time
of sorrow and stories and stories as they were told in twos.

One got way too old to stay that way too long. We were kids.
I worked the horse and grape. She worked at the foot
of the mighty mist. Now a damsel dark in cleaning smock

pours out from my phone. The air is neat.
The wind is swept. They took Ann by plane to Thunder Bay
and slept. She left without her hat.

Twitterpated

Her hat was found not far from the banks of the Tryst,
the familiar ring tone tripping softly off her mobile,
urges for survival in a year of twisting autumn

weather. Our acquaintance was brief and Bambi-like.
She had words for me, the woodlands slipping off her tongue.
She believed in ecstasy and forfeit, both

under pain of loss, the bend in the road ahead
all too strong an exile for a lonely boy like me.
But, hell, this might have been the middle of another lifetime

and her hat just another milestone, iconic in her hands—
tales of the fallen star, the brim of an apparent galaxy
doused in a river we had set to the max.

Museum Pieces: Galleria Borghese

I Canova's *Venus Victorious*

It takes time to raise an arm. To bend it so the stone's no thicker than a paper fold. So that we know the sky was once behind it.

Deception works its many miracles, time and wrinkles ironed out in polished marble. Just ask Canova.

That illusion in the Renaissance room was also 3-D shades of paint.

Everyone knows Venus was quite a lovely number in her day, venerable twists and turns of the female form included, but beauty comes with its own price tag.

Like anything in a life-size format, you can check it out at the gift shop.

II Bernini's *Truth Unveiled by Time*

Once we took holidays on our doorsteps. Daytime stay-at-home doo-dads in our pockets. Return tickets to the kitchen table and backyard benches.

Cheerios on our breath.

But with discounts, time, Bernini off the walls, the baroque of Truth herself could not keep us home.

Framed for all to see, the marble of the moon was sculpted in her eyes. Her thighs aglow with all that we'd been missing.

Duplicity suits the human voice, you said. Say, ah! Now, close your eyes and repeat. How many more days of this could we take?

And, oh, how we held hands—wands for magic occasions filled with possibilities, the truth unveiled by time.

She was dressed in standards. We were trimmed in futures.

III Caravaggio's *The Beheading of Saint John the Baptist*

Are you happy now?

Desktop

No big sky when you're in bed listening to the approximate drip of the rooftop rain, half-animal, half-Roman, and I'm of half a mind to text the nihilists next door and send them my very best ideas for getting old.

Sordid tales of *I told you so*, assorted bonbons of regret.

Accidents of birth, articles of faith, the list goes on.

Such words are brittle where they snap at the high- and low-lying branches, the winter rain that helps them wash away held up momentarily.

The rest of the night stays locked in place until the sun comes up on the screen and it's another image of the city that emerges, one I had quickly scrawled in words for winter, words for rain.

The Writing Life

The cornfield is not mandatory in my line of work, but just the same it's wonderful that it's there as I walk down the road, there, waking from its leaves, its sleep deep as green can get in the thick of a summer's blush.

The sky turns around to look at the field a second time as it does every day, much as I do when I walk up the road and return to the crops at my desk.

Manhattan Flattened: After the Sack of Rome

It was impossible to sit at Café Flor. We stood and peered over the ledge, all of ancient Rome, its ruins spread before us, tabletop happy, salt and pepper columns culminating at the very fringe of where Via Sacra met Google Maps dot com.

A marvel for sure, no doubt, not likely ever to be repeated quite like this again, although Manhattan flattened, circa 2000 CE, came to mind as we crossed against the red, the chariots burning up the track with their 2.6 litre engines.

Silence at a time like this seemed superfluous, yet all the same, given that our coordinates fixed in time and space were just this far from the sack of Rome, we thought it was altogether called for.

A Look Inside Cy Twombly's *Second Voyage to Italy*

Without too much makeup.

A map.

Without content or corners.

That's where he sent his goodbyes.

That's where the suitcase struck him on the head.

The world lurched forward on a happy note and he fell to his knees.

That's where he fell to his knees.

And the biscuit left crumbs on the floor.

The biscuit he took at the door before he left home.

The sky wasn't right so he fixed it and now it looks like !@#$%^&*.

He wasn't alone. Sybarites from the seven hills came to him in a dream.

One or two cubic metres of dirt per person.

That's where he stayed for the ink and italics.

That's where *adagio ma non troppo* took on different meanings.

That's where he clarified how much light to let in.

And certain ideas were mismatched in pairs.

And that's where he kept them.

Woman Declining Stairs (Suicide Bomber #2)

She'd rather elevate
on some other power.
If that's Manhattan,
she's not there
at 49th and Saks.
She's here. On the attack.
The outrage of some people,
of magazine tabloids
and their steeples,
of mortgages at prime.
The lady luck of yore's
long gone, long
before the GO Train
ever gets going—the two o'clock
at four and nowhere,
getting close, too close, to home.
She's late. She's dark.
She's wired.
Four pounds of nitro
fired with a spark and a four o'clock
fuse. Infused.
She's all God's children,
all in a matter of minutes.
She's Ella Fitz in broken bits,
a-tisket, a-tasket,
crushed to crumbs
like a handful of Triscuits.
She keeps no records.
She's disabused.
She has no use
for others who
do unto you
what she's had done to her.

And when she's gone,
she's gone for good.
But she'll be back
and you know it.
She's like the rain.
A cast of thousands.
Makes you think out loud.
Lose the crowd.

Daphne and Apollo: A Study Typed in Sentences
 —*after Bernini*

The Declarative

Daphne dips a foot into the marble pool, exfoliates, and shakes her breasts.

The sky is everything it's meant to be, an absence understood between the gods and the slightest mound she venerates, a kind of sacred oath she stands upon naked as the softest rain.

Dripping wet with light, her transparency is diaphanous as laurel boughs, her leaves so delicate and floral I can taste her breath inside my head.

The Exclamatory

Such a sky above those eyes! I could never leave her there so beautifully unnoticed!

The Interrogative

Who the hell does Apollo think he is, compromising kinetic beauty, that he, a god, could not keep his hands to himself and leave her truth untouched so that she must now transmogrify into a laurel in order to revisit what it's like to be in the arms of such a prick?

Was he such a prick?

The Imperative

You must find out.

PAINTER, Painter
—De Chirico, Piazza di Spagna

With his brush he had pictured the city holed up on his walls, stepping down a set of stairs, pruned and geometric. He didn't miss a thing. An angel here, a scoundrel there. Every flea in his neighbor's bed. He mistook the city for his books—icons, pillars for his palette. Light that old could only ever be imagined.

He painted word for word what he was told. He saw that the world is long. That it lasts a long, long time. That a city comes with titles. Gets reviewed. Copied. Forged and signed. He took one end of his canvas to match the other and kept on going, panel after panel.

Painted
the whole city in his head just like it was before he even got to see it up there on his walls.

Rosa Rosa Vagabonda

Waif.

Beached at doors. Bargain basement castaway. Sea life far from sea.

Inscapes of a beggar ferried on the Main, Via Santo What's-His-Name.

Thug.

A gypsy life at three.

Portrait of a cage pained and painted on her face.

Boxed.

Far from sea, far from ever seeing the painted sky.

Infant knows only what infant's shown. Eyes shut tightly opened wide.

Romanesque.

Hands behind her back. On her knees. *Polizia*-bound. Or bound by any other means.

Baby's born a second time when baby's found her name.

Remus, the Forgotten One

I remember the night of the birth: I was frail
though I would have said fraught at the time.

I remember what wonder felt when the queen had her babies, how
the wait was worth it, how Dad couldn't think for a week after that,
made up what he couldn't remember.

I remember quite a lot. I went to places for the very first time.
I was hungry; I suckled. I was tired; I slept.

So much of time went on in coffee shops, on cells, in the papers,
the hiss of the espresso maker, the chatter of cups I encountered,
someone stepping in, someone saying he was saddle-sore, shifting
and breaking as he went through his life.

I moved away.
I went looking for cottage favours in other people's places.
I met Americans.

In one voice I heard more rain than a city could bear.

A culture like *Stone Soup* came close to ideal, emboldened
to such a pitch everyone contributed whatever they could, but it failed.
It lacked a pinch of salt.

There were toll roads, runways to get in and, as expected,
admission fees to all the major sites.

But they were never meant for me.

I was Remus, the forgotten one.

I was the runt of the litter.

(Witness)

The air around Santa Maria across the Tiber tastes of pepper, paint, and menthols.

The crowds are lush and the horror of the night must be that it must end too soon.

Oh, the moon—another case of the vagrant moon.

No boats, no sails, no nightingales—no long and lasting life.

Just the moon and flowers left for little Claudio lost beneath the bridge.

Someone quotes St. Augustine to make it better—like mothers kiss the wound to help it heal.

Non c'è male, ma il dolore. There is no evil but pain.

Claudio's hat was all they found.

(A passerby in this city for whom the river coils and dreams, I step off the bridge, climb two sets of stairs, drink the wine I pour, wait for dinner among the petals of a marigold bright as sunflowers from the market, sit for artichokes and garlic at the table of *zi'* Maria, pasta plucked in a solo for guitars, and listen all the while to the music in a dish that re-invents the air on my side of the bridge.)

The Disquieting Muses
—after Mark Strand and De Chirico

They stand to wait much longer for eternity. Apollo's pawns are muted, waiting in the square where light will never interfere, and there is no need to see.

Some light, some shadow, a touch of darkness in the mist, but something's wrong. No one seems to know or care, they stand to wait much longer for eternity.

The sky's the colour of fog and filth, of smoke and windows, the mask of Guy Apollinaire. Where light will never interfere, there are no eyes to see.

Some light's the absence of a storm, the windows empty, static states where nothing moves, not a word up in the air. They stand to wait much longer for eternity.

Erect upon the edge, a light directly from some fantasy, the bright bulb of invention once was there. Where eyes will never interfere, they have no need to see

nor have the means, their faces blank, no one there to disagree, to break the wooden stance of nothing more to see. They stand to wait much longer for eternity.

Byron's Missing Fingers: Lessons from the Imagists

I
mothballed busted trussed-up statues
broken terracotta lips
desiccated limestone jackets
persistent as the classics

and here comes the sun recording its own passing

II
rundown ghetto
by the Tiber
made of temples and outside tables

headlines sightlines *Easy Rider* reruns
Scarface on the walls

and Domenico What's-His-Name
romantically inclined

III
noon bells ring from the Forum side

Rome in a room reflected onto a window
opening
where there's another window

compensating

IV
on a ledge the pen

that chips away
at some other shape
emerging from
another set of cloistered eyes

V
a fountain
a stroke of wilderness from the boreal land

moose head goose flesh turtle backs

backpacks

and as the sun would want it
oranges impaled on blades of grass

VI
the Tiber's on its side and sickly

coins in the mouth of the Trevi sour the clouds'
watery compositions

two people stranded at the gate
where the gate is shut

VII
Byron's missing fingers

on a trinity of strings and keyboard stops

in a piazza by the Virgin

in a piece by Piazzolla

in a crowded distant

twenty-first-century

version of himself

III

Roaming Charges—"Land Over Landings"

We were something of a passing
cloud, you and me
—bleak and heavy
      with assumptions.

Airborne, we left our friends behind,
burdened by impending runways
—a blight on their horizons
      to the east.

A shadow the size of a 747
now lands on the pop. of Whitevale
—and their eyes can't seem to meet
      the sky's.

Echo Lake

The rooster won't crow. There is no crow.
The land and the lake are chewable.
You pitch the fish out of the boat
and it sticks to butter. The leaves
are breathing so you can take a breather.
Those electric voices over the bay swallow children
whose feet go missing off the dock.
I taste vanilla in the air, burnt toast,
Joni Mitchell's cloudbanks.
Talk of real estate in the abstract
lands upon the land.

Some days are better than others.
Cargo becomes legendary: groceries, luggage
stuffed in paper bags, cottage-cooked and gulped.
Dog-strangler creeps in and out of a conversation,
puffs of Roundup, leafy greens and summer hues,
thoughts of a life next door
and a lake that comes bobbing in a bottle.
The corkscrew at the table sits among the empties.
Records of cottage life pick at the brain and
laughter is a godliness that can't compare.

Then, before you know it, a sixties sort of music
evaporating off the night-soaked ripples of the lake
reminds us that Herb and André,
Chris and Evie, still have mothers on this earth.

Can't Complain (Just Look at Detroit)

The people in Argentina look like the people of Argentina.

The Soviets are no more.

And gone the Beothuk.

Rome, as we know it, never would have perished without the Romans.

Yet, there's nothing in the mechanics of an assembly line that a Canova could not have sketched.

Now Tic Tacs rattle in the memory of my father's pockets. My mother's legs, such a cha-cha they could dance, the death rattle by and by.

Such dangers when you take a second chance at making history and then give up.

Can't complain though. *Jeudi* is to Thursday as often as it can be. Words like that stay put.

Family matters—it's the push-and-pull of memories that keeps us fit, the way neck muscles train for years to keep our heads above the ground.

I love a good finish, such as the day my uncle, Amadeus, bet on the ponies and the daily double took his heart.

The last notes I remember of his requiem hung above the Detroit River. I held my breath until the end.

At his funeral, my cousins and I laughed and laughed at the meaning of *terrestrial*, the earthlings that we are.

All the same, I was lonely in Windsor, a window with no one on the other side.

Coming in Friday to Windsor on Wednesday

A manual comes with every landing, fish oil and puddle-fat to polish the wings, waterproof the sun in our eyes.

Let us pray with both hands up in the air that we never touch bottom. Let us not get to know the jaws of Lake St. Clair.

The mice, tagged and numbered, scurry from seat to seat, feed on crumbs and chewing gum, tails tucked in an upright position.

People put up with enough to get above the clouds, cough ever so slightly into their mitts.

When was the last time you saw an angel all dressed up in polar fleece?

Or the last time a river took off like that, in a ribbon of grey steel?

Not on your life, especially when maps reduce the reach of possibilities, all the roads accounted for.

Coffee, spirits, building healthy communities at the Riverside Inn, I'm all for that. The way I see it, whether up or down, the world deserves better.

Just outside my window, the distance from here to there says that's Detroit.

Sure, smoke is rising where the sun should rise, but nothing's burning yet.

Envoy
　　—*for Tomaž Šalamun*

Crazy with December frost, the trees this morning buttoned up, rattled the icy wind with tendered arms.

The road was caked with salt.

This morning when I left the azure bits of sky behind, I saw for miles above, Air Canada to Windsor.

I saw what brief candle sparks an urge within to understand the tender-hearted poet on my lap.

He knows you can't get that level of Google precision for a shoreline that defines a lake by the window seat when the mind always changes its mind.

Are those baskets of the Food Bank I see beneath me, their handles toward mine eyes? Come, let me clutch them and give to the poor, the gap that sits between us only ever controlled by an engineer with a foot on the pedal.

A poet's work is never done. He feeds us from his donkey cart, the galley at the back of the plane. His words become the words that come between us.

This morning when the trees unflinched.

This morning when the road gave way.

The Tower

You fell from such a height,
just standing there, a jest, cruciform,
a mime that mirrored sky and all its contents
that long September day.
Then you left, you simply disappeared,
and we thought you'd gone for good.

We said we'd come back
for the raising of the girders,
see how you've been doing since.
Up on the CN once
we looked down past our feet to the city
where our feet had been.

Let's try that some day soon.

With hats upon our heads high above
the red and silver maples towering
where an open sky calypsos blue and clear,
we'll lean forward, both as one,
and make the wind come to us.

If a bench is on a bridge
and the bridge is meant to get across,
then the bench must be for something else.
We'll think of you that way.
Your height depends on where we stand.

Toying with the Above

The plane, drifting on a cloud of minor chords, lowered its head, cut through a beam of semi-languid light the sun had unleashed a hundred million years ago, and was only now rousing itself from the sleep it had preferred. It nodded into wakefulness, barely moved by the sudden change of states, began its descent into happiness at a precise forty-five-degree angle to the thoughts of its pilot.

The sun, perfectly in place and proud of what it stood for, came through the cabin window and sat in the aisles waiting like a patient poodle for the doors to open, caressing the feet of the passengers with connecting flights. It conjured destinations, spoke the names of fathers, mothers, Uncle Sam, and everyone knew them for the soothing hum of engines on the ground.

In and Out of Chatham

The bank that fed the world till now was on the other side.

The bank that bent the sky went bust.

The insides of the bus awoke with the scent of chips and curry.

The leather once on hoof now on a journey past the harvest.

The riders on their butts.

The bus that broke the beast and likewise runs on fours.

That fails. That forwards. That rears. That bears the grade.

The bank that bore the bus is at the station.

The Air in the Bus

Fossils of a two-pound hen fed to a trembling fire.

We mustn't fail, says the smoke in the next story.

Radio towers translate the dot to dot of roadside sequels. Elementary particles react like memes on the move. Cellular thoughts between the aisles catch on.

An act of trite contrition or slim starvation between stops.

A country song from the good old days that does no one no good.

We're ten miles out of reason. Your wife is bubbly. Her shoes are lovely.

That paper bag you opened fills the air.

A harvest big as dreams goes by.

The children, if there were children, wave.

A house appears beneath a roof.

The world renews itself every time the Greyhound stops.

London 2012

The corn is a blessing.

Along with the ministers of plenty, the general accounting in the fields, the act of getting it down to a simple stroke of fugues and figures, dollar for dollar, music to the ears.

The Bacchis, my neighbors, harbour the kinds of fundamentals that make us rich.

I am a sucker for the summer sounds I like, crickets and screen doors slamming; for a religion based on wars; a Monday morning abscess gone; "Greensleeves"; a box of Shreddies full to the brim behind a cupboard compost.

I remember London, the Olympic year of 2012.

I remember the fake verdant countryside and me in Vermont, the Middle Ages plain and simple, enchanted by the choirs, the fervour that consumed the passion.

And all the world nuts with the cosmic shower.

Pax Canadensis

The Romans conquered Upper and Lower Canada with a lash and wooden wheel. With a chalice made of bark.

They hovered in our history: loved to greet the morning air with a bite of fauna, loved to rein the forest in, gather rosebuds from the Shield.

They came to form the pillars for a heaven here on earth. To feel and feed the rain. Their frankincense was butter, tallow on a moonless night, the macadam of worship that came later.

Soon the place was all their brood, St. Clair and Bathurst, already a blend of mystics bleeding and handiwork that came with the work of rebuilding, the laying of bric-a-brac.

Around the corner from there, by Euclid Ave., where sons were born into manhood, the fertile frozen golden sod, there was marble for the taking made of fleeting wax and wings.

Goose down from The Bay.

The National Pantry

There's no grassier knoll than a grassy knoll.
A little red leaf detached from the sky falls to give birth.
The indigenous from down the country lane are stuffed
in sacs of flesh and soaked in blood.
Earplugs are tuned to the past. Roy Rogers
doubles bump into the prairies. From here,
the world is flat as the eye makes room for more.
Someone who bent himself into the shape of the wind
found a flowerpot standing in his place. Clouds
have an answer for everything, next day they're gone.
A sheepish look in the eyes of a wolf
that stands guard at the henhouse door.
The tomatoes and potatoes and the beans and the beets.
The aftershave perk of a linden tree by the driveway.
The Timbit on the nation's tongue.

Three Balconies

I
The kind of dust we get in Hamra,
our date palms in transition,
settles in profiles
of missing persons, passing times;
the kind of trust in clouds we fuss about
says we like to rehearse with the air,
seven stories from the sky,
and give a quick turn to the century
until no one's left but us it seems.

II
On Curzon, Riverdale South,
trees and siding,
trees and siding, yards
wide enough to contain
a pair of eyes and pin
the stars in place.
No more than that.
Summer seeping into
every leaf and pore.
The sky itself in pieces.

III
Destiny, brought to you by a right
on Gibbs, Tyrone Mills.
Air sweetened by a linden tree,
wild dust. Fiddleheads
and eastern phoebes.
Cedars in cathedral woods withstand
the evolution of pesticides,

a worldwide grief.
Triage and greener grass.
Green hope, young and growing:
the stubble of a grandson.

Poets on a Plane

August Kleinzahler

"Green Sees Things in Waves" reads significantly
better on Scotch, four or five shots with ice
in a plastic tumbler, full to the brim on ME212
bound for BEY from Charles de Gaulle
and the poem in my hands takes off,
begins to shoot sparks, kick and wiggle
something of a Broadway hit while I make
my way halfway down to the bottom of things
and I'm not thinking physics at this stage,
not even the physiology of Scotch on the senses,
just you and me, Mr. K., along for the ride
that's deep in my head and all shook up.
Honestly, your poetry may never get better
after this, the altitude altogether bracing
for the time of life we've been having,
vagaries of the soul in an afterlife and the unknown
quotidian march ahead of us matched
to the strange hours travellers keep in their cups.

Michael Ondaatje

Wish I had more time to fly,
to read him on this flight.
He could teach me a thing
or two about body parts,
where to put them
in a poem.

Take the inside
of an elbow,
the tender wrinkles
of padded flesh,
bent to shape a line, or
the long leg
left out in the aisle
before I find my way
back to another sigh.

Mary Oliver

I miss the trees,
the geese,
the explosive spring
that's not on this plane,
the ivy reaching
right up to the clouds
that don't seem so real
when you're in them,
at an altitude
your poetry has never
corrected
or left out
altogether.

Erin Mouré

Her wrist bones,
ankle bones, *chevilles*

chev'lure, a place in her hair

for the hair
and now

chevron

might be measured
as a diacritical sign—whereas Bly,
Enid Blyton

the book on her lap
{{a sign of wings to come}}

might take flight

leave us up in the air
two at a time

Carmine Starnino

I don't know you from Dante—
you're the other version of the island,
not the soporific one-note strum,
more the silver-peppered starlit bits
of night below. No slum intended. You're grist
for the mill, muled from place to place,
sentenced to make sense of double sense
and keep the poets' faith intact. Loose-
lipped, family-familiar, a match for Sunday
rides and change of on-location sites,
Via Santo This-and-That, the banks of the Saint
Lawrence going nowhere now without you.
You sucked at the tit of the she-wolf—a Roman
bro meant to mouth the words just so.

Ken Babstock

Hearty heartfelt turbulence the whole way, I borrowed
Berlin from your purse, stacked the towers of the
Kurfürstendamm on either side of the window seats,
slacked off on the beernuts.

When we landed one of us was already there—
soldiers, boots, poets in the squares,
one told the other all about matters of the in-between
as a middle-class hoax. Fred's
Not Here opened its doors
all of four hours and fifty-
seven minutes ago. I've never been.
All the same, let me stand you a drink
and tell me what you think.

James Tate

I look for contraband from the infinite
in the work of others, ducks in a tree,
tales of mishaps/shipshapes, insincerities
that gloss the fugitive crickets and their happiness,
slip-ups at the marvels of a spirit world
still stuck in the land of vapours, a sound
like distant thunder from the back of the plane,
but all I get are broken records, misspelled
ell-o-vees, the same old chronology of past events
'cause nobody makes it up like they used to
anymore. I'm up in the air with this son of a jet

and it tires me, for I am not getting any younger.
When, I wonder, will I be one with the couch again?
When, if I slumber, will the window seat
be more than a poem could ever intend?

There's a rooftop to my limits
and if I don't get a story out of this,
I don't know what I'll do.

Jump, perhaps. But what good is that
without pencil and paper to make it true.

North of Cochin

Ferry the locals from Kottayam to the church on Sunday.

Fetch the elephants.

Take the bus ride to Kumali,
come to the southwest corner
and the tea plantations, seven degrees south, overlooking
the ocean's scrim.
Mussels on request, unlimited rations of supplicants and sand.

$45 a day for two.

Albino dolphins and leopard-skin patches pad the beach.

All hats are cool.

Now you can forget how you got here.

Negotiate the sunset.

Nets in waiting above the sea.

Go to Giddyfly.

NOTES AND ACKNOWLEDGMENTS

- Epigraph by James Tate from *Worshipful Company of Fletchers* (The Ecco Press, 1994).

- "Hamra"
  A *dabke* is a traditional dance of the Middle East, popular in Lebanon. "La Mer" is Debussy's, but also Charles Trenet's of 1946 and, later, Bobby Darin's. Hamra is a neighbourhood in Beirut. The last words, of course, belong to Matthew Arnold's "Dover Beach."

- "Ballad from the Back of the Bus"
  The first line is John Lennon's from "The Ballad of John and Yoko."

- "Roaming Charges: Digs"
  Words in italics are Don DeLillo's from his novel, *Point Omega*.

- "A Look Inside Cy Twombly's *Second Voyage to Italy*"
  In 1957 Cy Twombly said about his work that each line he made was "the actual experience" of making the line, adding: "It does not illustrate. It is the sensation of its own realization." Years later, he described this more plainly. "It's more like I'm having an experience than making a picture," he said. Like some of these lines do for me.

- "Daphne and Apollo: A Study Typed in Sentences"
  After Bernini's sculpture of a similar title in the Galleria Borghese, Rome.

- "PAINTER, Painter"
  Giorgio de Chirico, Italian painter and writer, had an apartment on Piazza di Spagna in 1947. See *The Memoirs of Giorgio de Chirico* (Da Capo Press, 1994).

- "The Disquieting Muses"
  After Mark Strand's poem of that title inspired by De Chirico's painting of the same name, which also led to this poem. De Chirico painted so many different versions of the same piece that critics accused him of forging his own work.

- "Byron's Missing Fingers: Lessons from the Imagists"
  Lord Byron was no Imagist but he lived and wrote in Rome for a time. A statue to his memory at one of the entrances to the gardens of the Villa Borghese has several fingers missing on its writing hand, broken off by vandals one would think, or the passing years that certainly wear down all that's stone and solid. Written lines don't seem to suffer quite that fate at the hands of time. I can still read these lines as he wrote them, taken from Canto IV of his poem, *Childe Harold's Pilgrimage*:

  Of its own beauty is the mind diseased,
      And fevers into false creation:—where,
      Where are the forms the sculptor's soul hath seized?
      In him alone. Can Nature show so fair?
      Where are the charms and virtues which we dare
      Conceive in boyhood and pursue as men,
      The unreached Paradise of our despair,
      Which o'er informs the pencil and the pen,
  And overpowers the page where it would bloom again?

- "Roaming Charges—'Land Over Landings'"
  The agricultural lands around the hamlet of Whitevale in north Pickering are threatened by the coming of a new airport for Metropolitan Toronto, an airport that has been planned for decades and remains a contentious issue. Picket signs along the roads state the local population's opposition to this project quite bluntly as "Land Over Landings."

- "North of Cochin" is for André Renaud who, without knowing it, gave me this poem.

Some of these poems first appeared, sometimes in a different form, in *Descant*, *Exile*, *Grain*, *Prairie Fire*, *Arc*, and *Rusted Radishes* (Beirut).

Heaps of thanks to Rania Jaber, Mishka Mourani, Susan Briscoe, Kitty Lewis, Barry Callaghan, Barry Dempster, and all the bloggers and critics who take the time to read and review our books. And thanks to Alayna Munce, copy editor at Brick, whose attention to detail has put a polish on so many of these lines. Special thanks to my editor, Nick Thran, meticulous and generous, who more than anyone helped this book become what it is. And to Ann, who makes of our world together an incomparable comfort zone.

ANTONY DI NARDO is a poet and teacher. He currently divides his time between Beirut, Lebanon—where he teaches English at International College—and central Canada. He is the author of two previous collections of poems: *Alien, Correspondent* (Brick Books, 2010) and *Soul on Standby* (Exile Editions, 2010).